Up Against an Oak Log: Rotting

Ayla Jones

Up Against an Oak Log: Rotting © 2023
Ayla Jones

All rights reserved.

No part of this publication may be reproduced, stored in a retrieval system, or transmitted, in any form or by any means, electronic, mechanical, photocopying, recording or otherwise, without the prior written permission of the presenters.

Ayla Jones asserts the moral right to be identified as author of this work.

Presentation by *BookLeaf Publishing*

Web: www.bookleafpub.com

E-mail: info@bookleafpub.com

ISBN: 9789357441193

First edition 2023

PREFACE

Up against an oak log: rotting.
Stoop beneath the top soil potting;
Where roots delve down deep,
Atop lie things to eat.
In some way morbid;
Yet naturally distorted.
I hope to find myself there,
Up against an oak log: rotting.

Roots

I grew up in the deep south, the old south.
Live oaks weighed down with Spanish moss.
Stained histories of antebellum mansions,
Reupholstered in pursuit of future memories.

The best time of year
Was when the honeysuckles bloomed.
The air was ambrosial, hazy, and yellow,
Blanketed in pollen, our springtime snow.

It stormed loudly.
Pounding thunder shook the Earth,
Trees shuddered at the sound.
Only the strong held their ground
Against that mighty authority.

Water flooded clover filled lawns
And I marched,
Proudly stomping my feet
In newly discovered lakes.
Georgia red clay stained my being.
That famous sediment,
A wetland sentiment mixed in.
Lakes became swamps.

It was torrid summers and mild winters.
Fields of fireflies, cicadas, and katydids.
An orchestral performance every sunset,
Cacophonous, orchestral.

The air was as thick as warm honey.
Not as viscous but just as sticky.
Oppressive, still, dense, weighted, stuffy.
A million microscopic drops frozen in time
Clung to fabric and skin alike.

Tangible and invisible,
Like the fondness
And nostalgia that settles
In my soul when I remember
The deciduous forest,
Dais for infinite imagination.

Too Much

In some ways
I feel like a wild pot-bellied animal
Lying in a field in the savannah.
Entrails dripping through the grass
With the pregnant knowledge of what
That malicious laughter coming from the
Underbrush means.
Those eyes are equipped to pierce through
The black veil of night
Surrounding a meal they know can't fight back.
I hear them stalk toward me.
I stare at the moon and feel the wind
Cool against my hide.
Everything goes quiet.

They pounce,
Silent as a ghost.

The moon fades from my vision as my
Exposed lungs take one
Last shuddering, crepitating breath.

Hyenas are known
To completely finish their prey.
So why

Do they
Never finish
Eating me?

I'm being eaten alive.

Paranoia

I think they saw me.
They saw me.
Saw me laying there,
I think.
'How do you know if they saw?'
I think to myself laying
On the ground.
I saw them,
Watching me
Watching them
Watching each other
Thinking to ourselves,
Did they see me?

I think they know
I'm thinking of them
Thinking of me
Watching each other
Watch each other.

I think they saw me.
I saw them.

Time curse

Linear and somehow round.
Oh, how you bend to haunt me.
A moment.
A minute.
A day.
You mangled barbed wire
Stabbing me in the back.
I hope you whither away in the same fashion
In which you came into existence.
And yet,
You keep moving
In ways
That will evade me until
I take my last breath.
And as you claim another soul,
My soul,
Know that I hated
Every second
You bent to your will.

Reflection

Stare.
Whisper.
Sharp-tongued quips,
Inaudible, overheard.
She doesn't care.
Tastes bitter.
A bad trip.
Blurred.

She agrees?

Vile, violent thing
Curled up in a corner
Not to meet an eye.
Superior and inferior.
Waltzing tightrope strings
between present and former.
Logic defied,
Bilinear, off balance.

How can such a wretched walker
Walk among the many?

I hate her,
She hates me.
An ouroboros of
Mistrust and understanding.
In all her grandeur
She missed the chance to see
She and me is us
A loop of mishandling.

The Move

The desire to run eats me,
Bites my ankles at every step.
Knawed its way into my brain,
The thought won't let me rest.
Im ready to sprint
Halfway across this world
Barefoot and bleeding
If that's what it takes
To take me from here.
I'm ready to lie down
And never move again
If the opportunity
Slips from my grasp.
I find it hard
To find peace
In this place.
Am I a coward if I go?
Am I a martyr if I stay?

Wyoming Weather

A whisper of the night flows into my exposed
windowsill,
And the sky lets go of her agony for just one night.
Her thunderous cries heard across the vast lonely
yellow.
Her tears feeding the earth, her lover, she years to
touch again.
I am lost in their tragic love.

I feel
Every
Atom
Of my being swell with the desperation they feel so
deeply it writes history.

Then,
The noise comes back.
Once again I am not some witness to an event greater
than me.

I am just a girl
Sitting in her room
Watching a thunderstorm

Thinking in metaphors.

Baggage

Let it go.
Weight of the world, heavy as it is, can crumble
in your hands.
Atlas had no better hold than you.
Drop it; freedom is all it craves.
Ascend above it and be weightless to this world.
Depart with the knowledge that you escaped.

Growing Self Awareness

It's confusing
As it grows,
Pushing.
A breath, a single hitch.
A fire lights, ticklish.
No more excuses.
It's become too self-aware to ignore,
Useless to dismiss.
An elephant,
With an eye in his mouth.
The sun, who was eaten by buddha.
Its warmth, his love.
Conversing with a comet
Who can tell you stories
Of worlds yet discovered.

Masks

Burning never felt so satisfying
And I can't feel my toes.
The paint is dripping off the walls
In slow sludging sacks.
It can't be stopped,
Or helped.
Trust me I've tried.
I've painted these walls a thousand times.
The walls reject it.

Melts right off
Congealing on the floor.
Stains my ankles,
False colors.
It's hard to wade through
This half dry ocean of lies.
Clings to me like
I owe it more than it's already taken.

If I stop painting,
Will this pond dry,
Cementing me to the floor,
Paralyzing me from change?
Or will I be able to walk freely
Without fighting

Every step of the way?
Maybe I can wash
The paint off my feet
And take a clean step forward.

I Can't Sleep

I'm walking
On a concrete path
I think.
Walking to where?
When?
Is that a crack in th-

Sleep.

I was asleep.
Sitting up disoriented and weird,
Eyelids heavy in contradiction
Of my freshly risen consciousness.
I was definitely asleep.
For all of twenty-seven minutes
And thirty-eight seconds.
That's what the clock told me
When I asked.

Sleep.

It's been avoiding me for a while now.
I close my eyes to catch a glimpse
Of that never-ending abyss.
Total relinquishment

Of mind and body.
As I'm walking toward it,
I always trip right back into awareness.

Sleep.

I ask myself,
"Who needs it anyway?"
My eyelids wage their war.
Some tired, battle-worn squid
Drags my mind back into the deep.
Its ink painting my sight black.

Sleep,

What relief.

Unhealthy Habit

Sleep deprivation,
Counting sheep like
Some cheap trick will
Cure my desperation.

Ode to the lullaby
Whose notes attempt
To soothe my mind;
A fruitless war cry.

Under my eyes
Lies proof of the problem,
Freely shares state secrets,
Prevents me from lies.

Daydreams become
Half-awake trances,
Where foggy focus
Becomes blurry numbness.

Sleepwalking into every room,
Tiptoeing into unintentional meditation,
Tripping into neverending circles,
Falling to my own doom.

Sometimes I wonder
What I would be like
If I attempted to fix
My habitual blunder.

I find myself in these sleepless hours,
More real than the zombie that
Hobbles around in the daytime;
That perpetual wallflower.

Dreams Inside of Dreams

Often when I wake, Im confused.
Am I really awake?
When the clock chimes, Im doomed.
Often when I wake, Im confused.
I'll admit, my suspicion is reused.
Oh for goodness sake!
Often when I wake, Im confused.
Am I really awake?

Recurring Themes

Being chased.
Running away.
Tripping through
A dreamscape
Confused.
Subconscious repetition
In every edition.
Some higher power
Replaying a message,
A warning,
Advice?
Escape evades
Another maze.
Always running.
From what?
I wonder.

How can I stop running
When I don't know what I'm running from?

On the other hand
Maybe im running toward something.

Sprinting,
Exhilarated,
Unwavering adrenaline
Carrying me to
Some unclosed
Destination.
A race of
Predestined fate
Making me
Accelerate
Lacking the
Exhaustion,
Sweat, fear,
And shame
Of not coming
In first place.

Confirmation Bias

Belief is a funny thing.
A nonsensical, comforting thing
That allows the believer
To find any form of validation
For their hopes, dreams, and misfortunes.
The funny part is that it can go any way.

I believe it will get better
I believe they're out to get me
I believe that God is on my side
I believe there is no God
I believe in evolution
I believe in creationism
I believe I'm good
I believe I'm evil
I believe I need help
I believe people are helpless
I believe the Earth is flat
I believe flat Earthers are ignorant
I believe I'm right
I believe I'm wrong
I believe in humanity
I believe humanity is ruining everything
I believe in hard work
I believe hard work is pointless

I believe I can become smart
I believe I was born stupid
I believe in my country
I believe my country is terrible
I believe in traditions
I believe in reformation
I believe in aliens
I believe we're the only ones in the universe
I believe I'm the hottest one in the room
I believe I'm ugly and unlovable
I believe in global warming
I believe global warming is a hoax
I believe in the medical industry
I believe in a holistic lifestyle
I believe men and women are equal
I believe in the patriarchy
I believe this is pointless
I believe I'm making a point

I believe, I believe, I believe.
Our beliefs create our person,
Our person looks for information
To validate our beliefs.
Choose yours wisely.
True or false,
You will always find proof
For what you choose to believe.

Aquinas believes in a God

Motion mono mover,
Multispectral microanalysis,
Masterstroke multiverse,
Metamorphic metaphysics,
Most masterful micromanagement,
Manipulated material,
Made miraculously.
Mythological moderator.

Efficient cause
Effectively enunciates
Extraordinary elaborateness.
Endless expressionistic
Enormousness encapsulates
Etherial eternalness.

Contingency concentrates
Circumstantial chance.
Conundrum creation,
Clandestine civilization,
Chronological classification,
Cognitive contemplation.
Consequential consciousness.

Perfection personified
Predates people.
Philosophical participation,
Psychological polarization,
Predetermined predictable
Placement provides proof.
Perceptive perspective.

Design dictates
Demonstrability.
Draftsmanship development,
Descriptive decoration,
Dictatorial dematerialization,
Devotional developer.
Dreaming diety dedication.

On The Topic of Religion

I was raised Christian,
Baptist moved pentecostal
Moved to some ambiguous
'Yes I believe but not what you're preaching'.

How many times was the bible translated?
How many words have been changed
Purposefully to support
Specific politics, themes,
Beliefs, and ideologies?

Logically, I can't take
What's written at face value.
Logically, there has to be a God.

There is good in some
Stories,
Morals,
Philosophies,
Ideas
To take away
To be a good person.

The problem lies with people
Who are only good for the sake
Of getting into heaven.

When you're only good
To accept goodness in return
You have the wrong intentions.

All of us, same as the sinner
Judged last Sunday
In the house of the Lord.

Observation and acceptance
Over judgment and unfairness.

True spirituality is being good
Without the threat of eternal damnation,
Without selective participation in
mistranslations.
Don't take God's name in vain.

Legacy

Uninspired.
Conspiratorial.
Is it the end?
A beginning?
Will it ever end?
Has it already started?
I can never tell.
I can say this,

Outcome omitted,
I'll still be alive
Breathing poison,
Drinking contamination,
Eating chemicals,
Rotting from the inside
Just like everyone else.

We're all the same
Nixing defining characteristics,
Absent in soul.
A body remains
Feeding the Earth.
Maggots, worms,
Mushrooms, roots
Gorge themselves
In the antithesis of youth.

Will my poisoned body
Poison the Earth
Even in death?
Should I feel guilty about that?
I don't.

An inevitability.
A culmination of humanity.
Greedy, selfish,
Power hungry, angry
Humanity.

I hope we become
More than the legacy
We're currently writing.

I worry
We'll never be
Anything more
Than a contradiction.

Hoping for Purpose

In the spirit of being hopeful,
Prayer of hope in the full,
Which often makes me feel like a fool,
I spend my time writing.

Hope has a way
Of pulling you toward its fire,
Thawing out the icy threads
Needled into fiber of flesh,
Cross stitched into
Existence with the insistence
That nothing is worth it.

It melts the iron shackles
Bound and bolted to my ankles,
Halting every attempt to make
A single step in any direction.
Possibility of endless possibilities
Slipping in the folly of my own imagination.
Imagine my indignation
When all it took to free me is hope.

If thoughts shape reality
And I'm inclined to think they do,
Then I think my thoughts

Are as outlandish as you.
In all probability
The possibility of becoming yourself
Is one in four hundred quadrillion.
Thinking thoughts that rare
Ought to change my forlorn disposition.

But hope isn't rare.
Maybe it is these days.
Or maybe, more than this,
I think we think about having hope
Without a willingness to confront the emptiness
That guts you before hope
Burns up all the space it left behind.
A cavern of new potential,

One I intend to fill with words.

The Net

I find peace in the prospect of finality,
Though the futility of waiting for it
Is almost as grand as the ending itself.
Does anything ever really end?

A more likely explanation
Is a continuation,
Neverending transference
From one thing to the next.

Blade of grass
To the dragonfly
Lazing on the lotus
Or else zipping by.

I think I've been them all.
You and I, an infinitesimal,
Microscopic speck.
Strings in the same net.

Cast through all
Space and time,
Wielding a gravity
Both heavy and divine.

Every knot, convergence
Of what I have been
And all I ever will be
Before and after this life's end.

Freefall

I stand, on the edge of a cliff;
Watching growing waves
Crash into the limestone.
Stealing facets back into the sea,
It slowly climbs its way to me.
If I stand still long enough,
The ground beneath my feet will fall.
Weathered into fine-grain sand,
It returns home.
The sea could swallow me whole,
If I stand still long enough.
A seagull flies overhead
And I am filled with jealousy
For the ease that bird displays
Flying over ocean spray;
Without concern,
Without doubt.
If I stand still long enough,
He'll get away.
Setting sun,
Dipping just below the horizon line.
Pressure swelling;
Compelling me to make a decision
Before the moon rise.
If I stand still long enough,

I'll have missed my chance.
I plan to move before then;
Before I'm eaten alive,
Before it's too late.
I've grown tired of standing still.
Flying or falling,
Either way, I'm jumping.
I'll land where I'm meant to.

www.ingramcontent.com/pod-product-compliance
Lightning Source LLC
LaVergne TN
LVHW010945200726

843509LV00013B/2289